Egyptian Collection Counted Cross Stitch

by Juliet Foster

Supporting the MS Society

Juliet Foster

Text, images and designs ©2012 Juliet Foster
All rights reserved. This publication may not be reproduced, stored in a retrieval system, or transmitted, in any form or by any means, electronic, mechanical, photocopying, recording or otherwise, without the prior permission of the author.

ISBN-13: 978-1475211290
ISBN-10: 1475211295

If you experience any problems with this book or the designs within it, please contact egyptian@julietfoster.co.uk

This book is dedicated to my Mum, Ann, love and miss you every day and to my sister Isabel for her faith in me – love ya kiddo.

Juliet Foster

Acknowledgements
A huge thanks you to Isabel Foster for imparting her expert knowledge at the crucial moment. Much appreciated, Isabel, I bow to your superior skill.

Thanks also to Jeff Piper for his invaluable help eliminating glitches – thanks for being my spare (working) pair of eyes, Jeff!

Contents

- Introduction by the author ... 6
- How to stitch these charts ... 7
- Eye of Horus ... 8
  - Dimensions ... 8
  - Shopping List ... 8
  - Eye of Horus Key ... 9
  - Eye of Horus Chart ... 10
- Heh, God of Mischief ... 11
  - Dimensions ... 11
  - Shopping List ... 11
  - Heh, God of Mischief Key ... 12
  - Design Notes ... 12
  - Heh, God of Mischief Chart ... 13
- Ibis and Baboons ... 15
  - Dimensions ... 15
  - Shopping List ... 15
  - Design Notes ... 16
  - Ibis and Baboons Key ... 16
  - Ibis and Baboons Chart ... 17
- Egyptian Sampler ... 19
  - Dimensions ... 20
  - Shopping List ... 20
  - Egyptian Sampler Key ... 21
  - Design Notes ... 22
  - Egyptian Sampler Chart ... 23

Juliet Foster

Introduction by the author

This book has been a long time in the making, designs compiled over years of tinkering with ideas. Each motif in this book is unique and based on original sources, things I've seen or books I've read. Where this might be of interest, I've added a little bit of information with the chart.

All proceeds from the sale of this book are donated to the MS Society, a charity very close to my heart. If it hadn't been for MS, I would never have started designing, so it seems only right that any royalties raised should go toward research and support.

I hope you enjoy stitching the designs as much as I enjoyed creating them.

How to stitch these charts

1. Find the centre of your fabric by folding it in half horizontally and then vertically. Using the arrows on the motif chart, locate the start point.

2. Work the cross stitch in two strands of cotton, following the key.

3. Once you have completed the cross-stitch, work the backstitch in one strand of cotton.

4. Check your work over for mistakes and missed stitches before preparing it for mounting.

Note: Some charts in this book stretch over multiple pages. Where this occurs, notes specific to the chart in question explain the orientation in relation to your stitching.

Juliet Foster

Eye of Horus

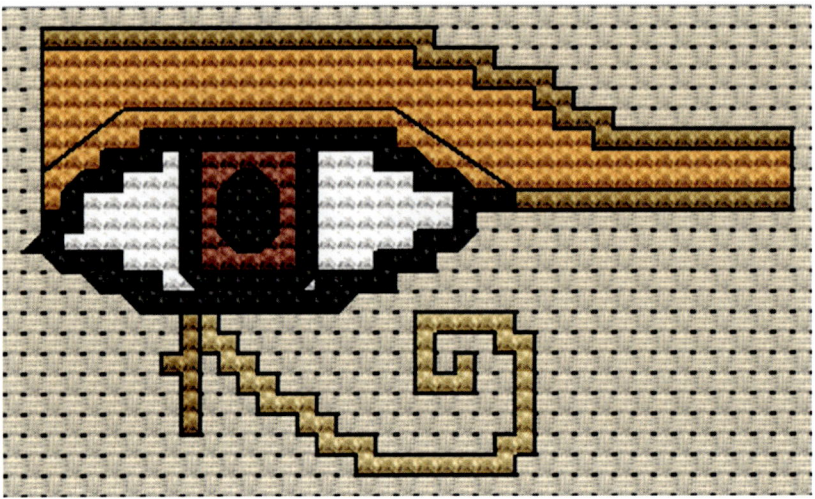

This simple motif uses whole and fractional stitches to complete the well-known Egyptian symbol of protection and good health. It features in the Egyptian Sampler on page 19 and is included here in a separate motif as the most popular design to stitch on its own. At 40x 22 stitches, it's perfect for cards and gifts.

Dimensions

40 x 22 stitches

Shopping List

- Aida/Evenweave of a size and colour to suit the design area
- Stranded Cotton as listed in key
- Size 24 tapestry needle
- Mount to suit the size of the design on your chosen fabric

Note: The pictured design was stitched using DMC stranded cotton. Although the closest alternatives are listed, other cottons may not produce the same results.

Eye of Horus Key

DMC	Anchor	Madeira		
Cross stitch in two strands				
3852	907	2210	■	
B5200	1	2402	●	White
3046	887	1414	▼	Yellow beige - med
832	907	2104	◇	Golden olive
3031	380	1904	◆	Mocha brown – v dk
918	351	2008	◤	Red copper - dk
310	403	1810	◢	Black
Backstitch in one strand				
918	351	2008		Red copper - dk
310	403	1810		Black

Juliet Foster

Eye of Horus Chart

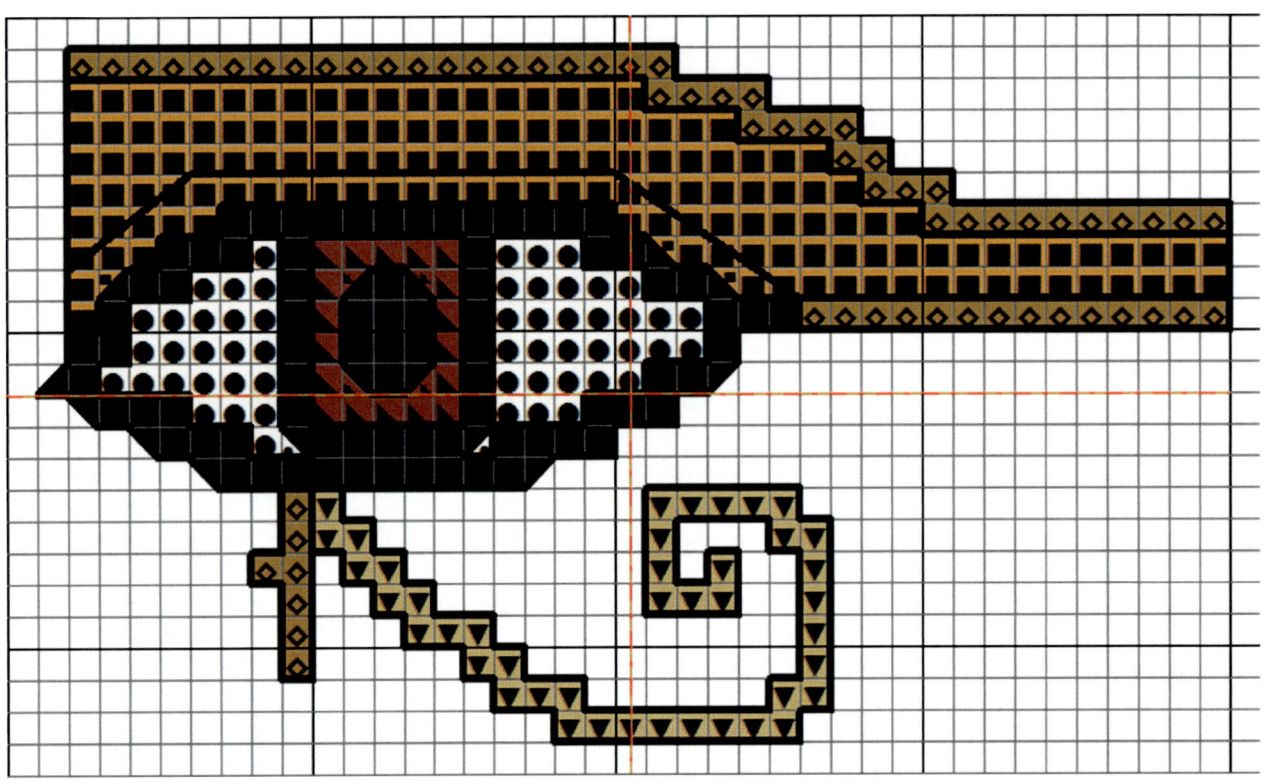

Heh, God of Mischief

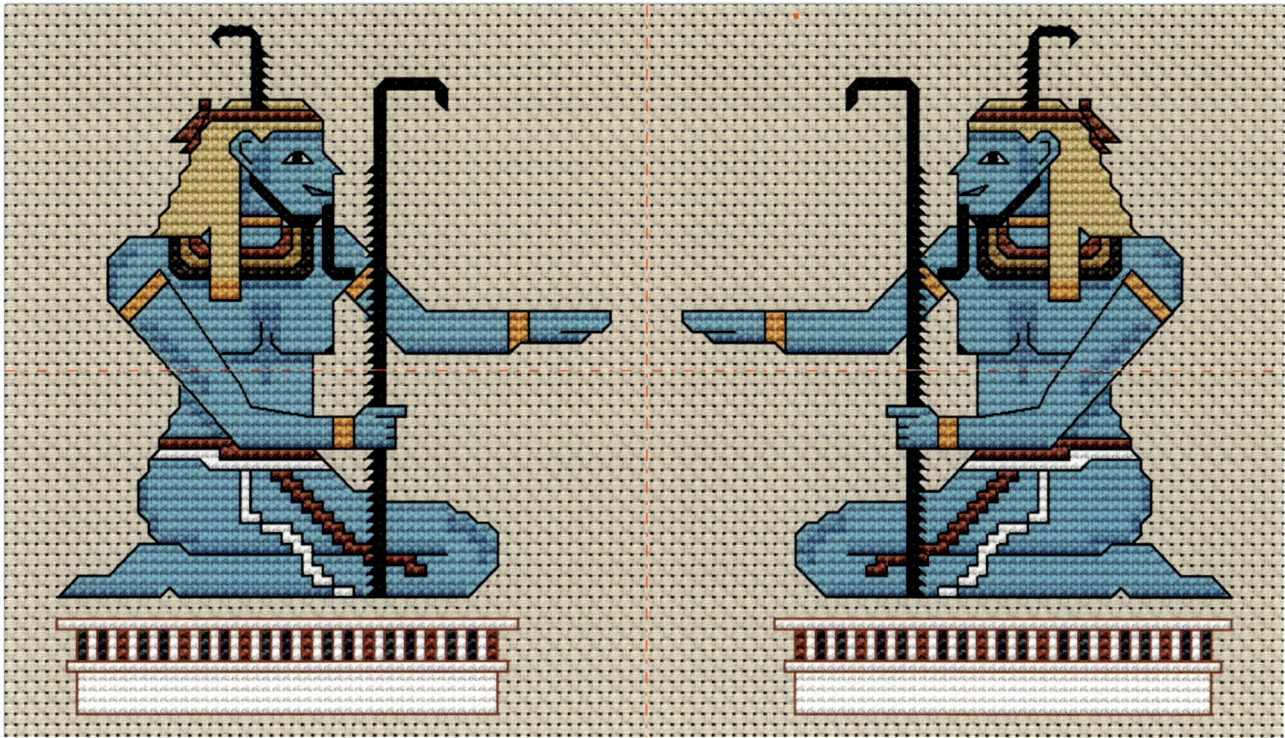

This bold motif is based on an illustration of Heh found in the Egyptian Book of the Dead. It appears later in the Egyptian Sampler chart, however he is such a popular design in his own right that I've charted him separately giving the dimensions and key needed just for him.

Dimensions

Stitch one or both motifs:

- One motif - 54 x 65
- Both motifs - 115 x 65

Shopping List

- Aida/Evenweave of a size and colour to suit the design area based on fabric count
- Stranded Cotton as listed in key
- Size 24 tapestry needle

Note: The pictured design was stitched using DMC stranded cotton. Although the closest alternatives are listed, other cottons may not produce the same results.

Heh, God of Mischief Key

DMC	Anchor	Madeira		
Cross stitch in two strands				
3852	907	2210	▽	
3865	1	2402	◢	White
3046	887	1414	✕	Yellow beige - med
832	907	2104	⊙	Golden olive
3031	380	1904	⋈	Mocha brown – v dk
918	351	2008	♥	Red copper - dk
310	403	1810	■	Black
3846	433	1103	●	
3844	410	2506	Z	
561	212	1312	⌛	Jade – v dk
3750	1036	0914	⌛	Antique blue – v dk
Backstitch in one strand				
918	351	2008		Red copper – dk
310	403	1810		Black

Design Notes

Backstitch on the Heh figure is completed in black. Backstitch around the plinth is completed in Red copper.

Heh, God of Mischief Chart

Left facing

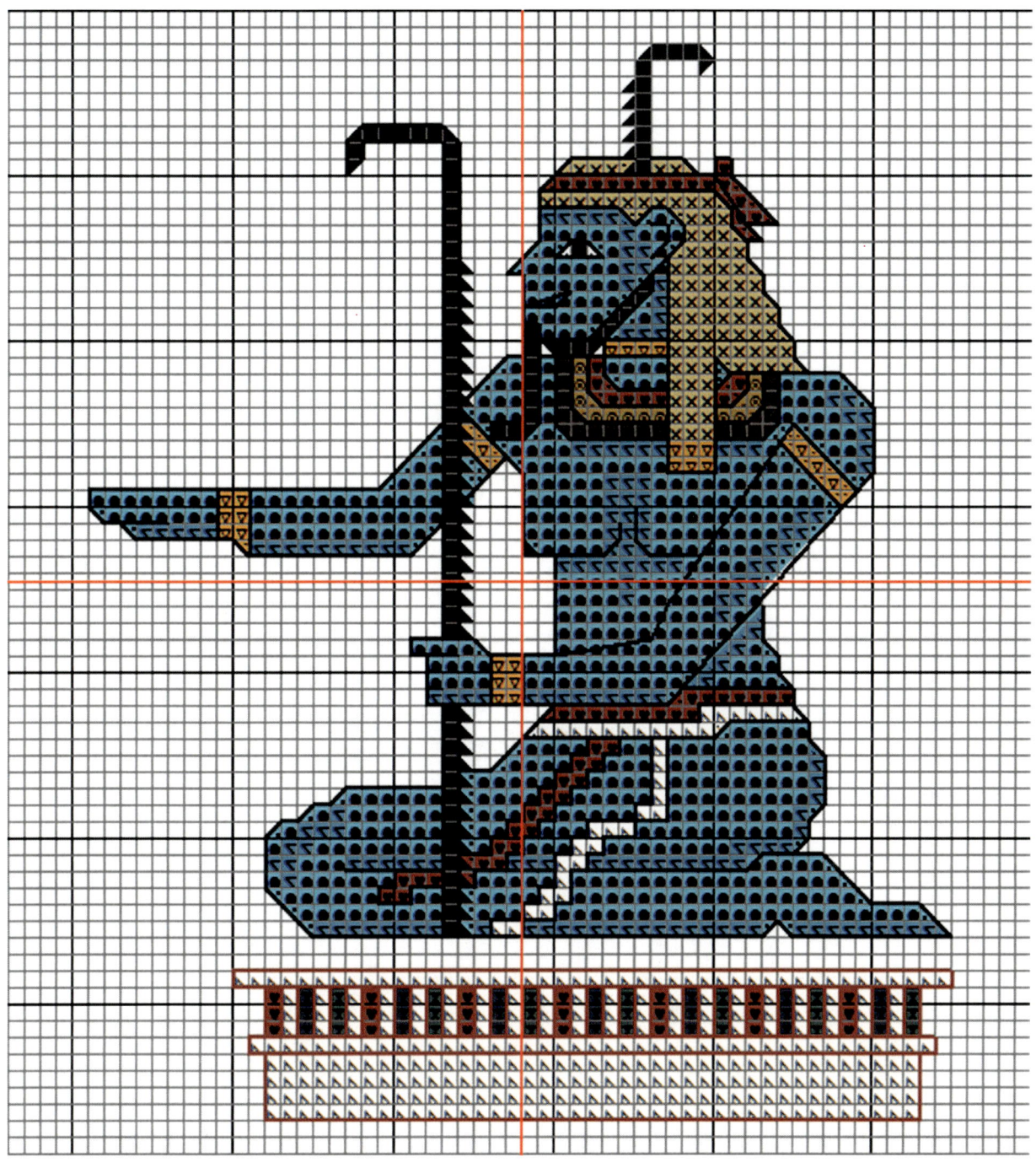

Juliet Foster

Right facing

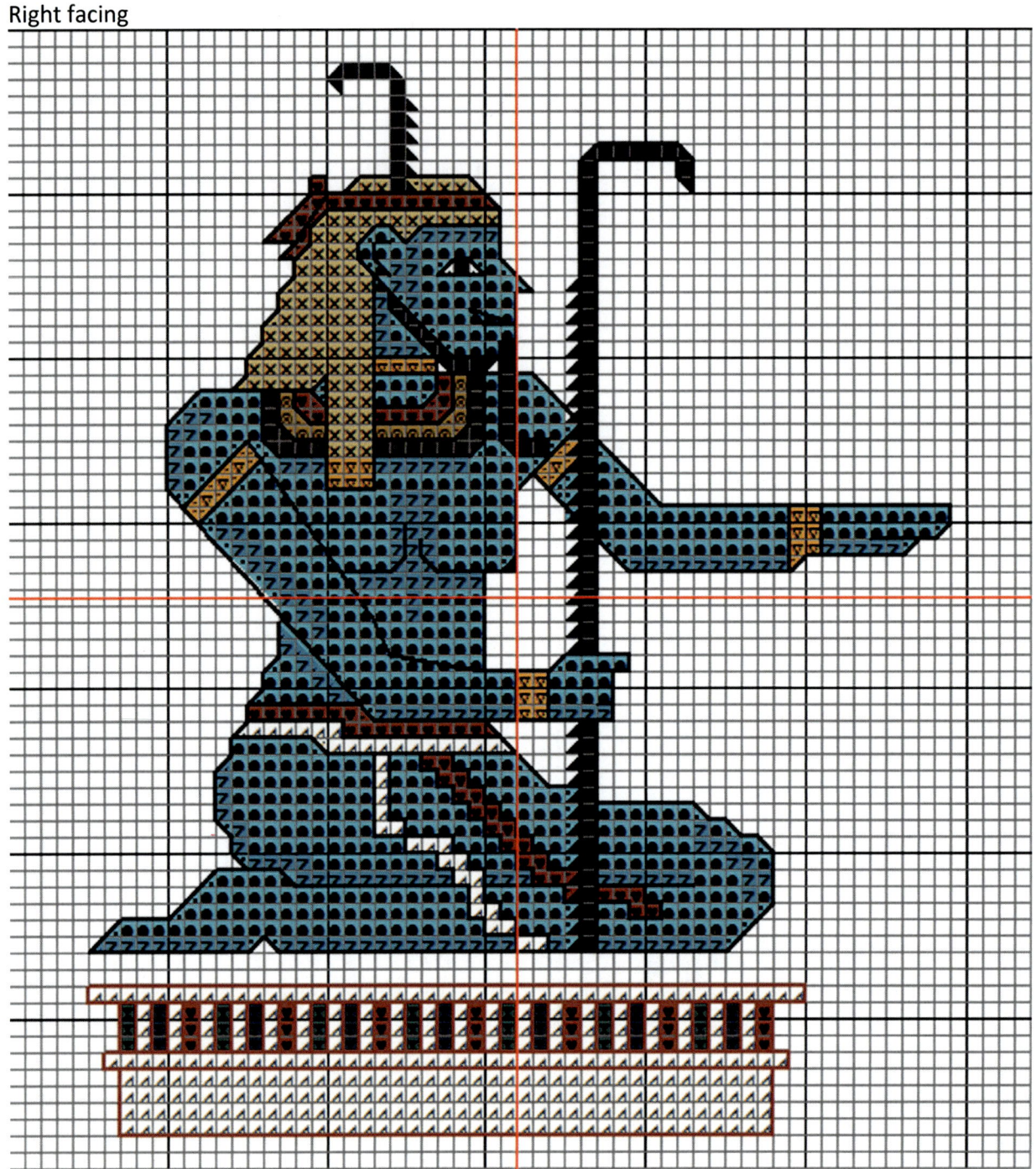

Ibis and Baboons

The ibis and the baboon were sacred to the Ancient Egyptians and feature strongly in the Book of the Dead. To save you locating them in the Egyptian Sampler Chart pages where they are split, the motifs are charted separately here.

Dimensions

- Ibis – 28 x 47
- Baboon – 13 x 13

Shopping List

- Aida/Evenweave of a size and colour to suit the design area based on fabric count
- Stranded Cotton as listed in key
- Size 24 tapestry needle

Note: The pictured design was stitched using DMC stranded cotton. Although the closest alternatives are listed, other cottons may not produce the same results.

Juliet Foster

Design Notes

To maximise the clarity of symbols, the ibis and baboons left-facing are charted separately to right-facing and arranged differently to the introductory image.

All backstitch is completed in black. If you have any difficulty in distinguishing the symbols in fractional stitches, use the backstitch line to guide you. Fractional stitches are worked in the same colour as whole stitches in a block delimited by backstitch. The baboon eye is a ¾ stitch in black. The ibis eye is also a ¾ stitch in black; however the backstitch picks up the white from the surrounding block to form the white of the eye.

Ibis and Baboons Key

DMC	Anchor	Madeira		
Cross stitch in two strands				
3852	907	2210	∇	
3865	1	2402	●	White
3046	887	1414	✗	Yellow beige - med
832	907	2104	▼	Golden olive
3031	380	1904	⊙	Mocha brown – v dk
918	351	2008	⋈	Red copper - dk
310	403	1810	♥	Black
561	212	1312	z	Jade – v dk
Backstitch in one strand				
310	403	1810		Black

Ibis and Baboons Chart

Left facing

Juliet Foster

Right facing

Egyptian Sampler

Each motif in this sampler is taken from the Egyptian Book of the Dead or The Book of Going Forth by Day, also known as the Papyrus of Ani. It describes all of the prayers and rituals that the Ancient Egyptians believed were necessary in order for a soul to reach the afterlife. The motifs are all to be found decorating the tombs of the Pharaohs.

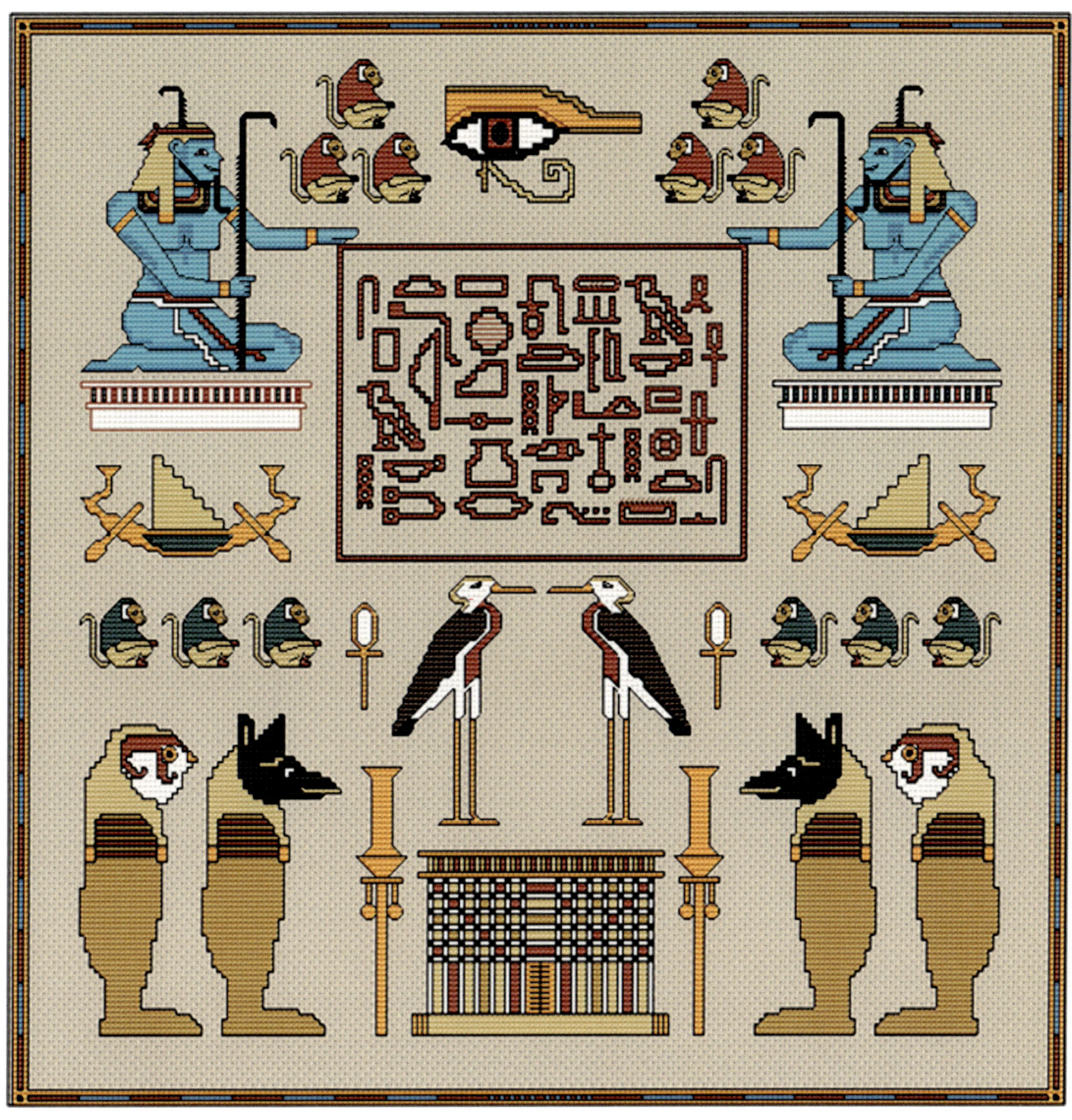

Juliet Foster

Dimensions

206 x 206 stitches

14HPI – 37.5 x 37.5cm (14.75 x 14.75in)
16HPI – 33 x 33cm (13 x 13in)
18HPI – 29.5 x 29.5cm (11.5 x 11.5in)

Shopping List

- Aida/Evenweave of a size and colour to suit the design area
- Stranded Cotton as listed in key
- Size 24 tapestry needle
- Mount to suit the size of the design on your chosen fabric
- Frame with minimum aperture of 29.5 x 29.5 cm (11.5 x 11.5 in)

Note: The pictured design was stitched using DMC stranded cotton. Although the closest alternatives are listed, other cottons may not produce the same results.

Egyptian Sampler Key

DMC	Anchor	Madeira		
Cross stitch in two strands				
3852	907	2210	■	
B5200	1	2402	●	White
3046	887	1414	▼	Yellow beige - med
832	907	2104	◇	Golden olive
3031	380	1904	◆	Mocha brown – v dk
918	351	2008	◣	Red copper - dk
310	403	1810	◢	Black
3846	433	1103	◣	
3844	410	2506	⊔	
561	212	1312	□	Jade – v dk
3750	1036	0914	○	Antique blue – v dk
Backstitch in one strand				
3031	380	1904		Mocha brown – v dk
918	351	2008		Red copper – dk
310	403	1810		Black

Juliet Foster

Design Notes

So that symbols are clear and not compacted, the Egyptian Sampler chart is divided into sections. The following 9 pages show the sections of the sampler beginning with the top left-hand corner. Section 2 follows on vertically from section 1. Section 4 returns to the top of the design. The pattern is shown in this table:

1 (page 23)	4 (page 26)	7 (page 29)
2 (page 24)	5 (page 27)	8 (page 30)
3 (page 25)	6 (page 28)	9 (page 31)

Where a section cut falls along a backstitch line, so that the backstitch can be seen clearly, the next row or column of squares is picked up slightly. All motifs are outlined in backstitch. Most is completed in black; however there are some areas where mocha brown or red copper is specified. For example, cross-hatching lines within hieroglyph symbols are worked in red copper.

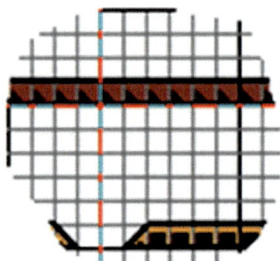

The exact centre of the design falls in section 5 on page 27. You can choose to begin stitching with any section as with any chart you work from. The centre is located by following the broken red line.

Egyptian Sampler Chart

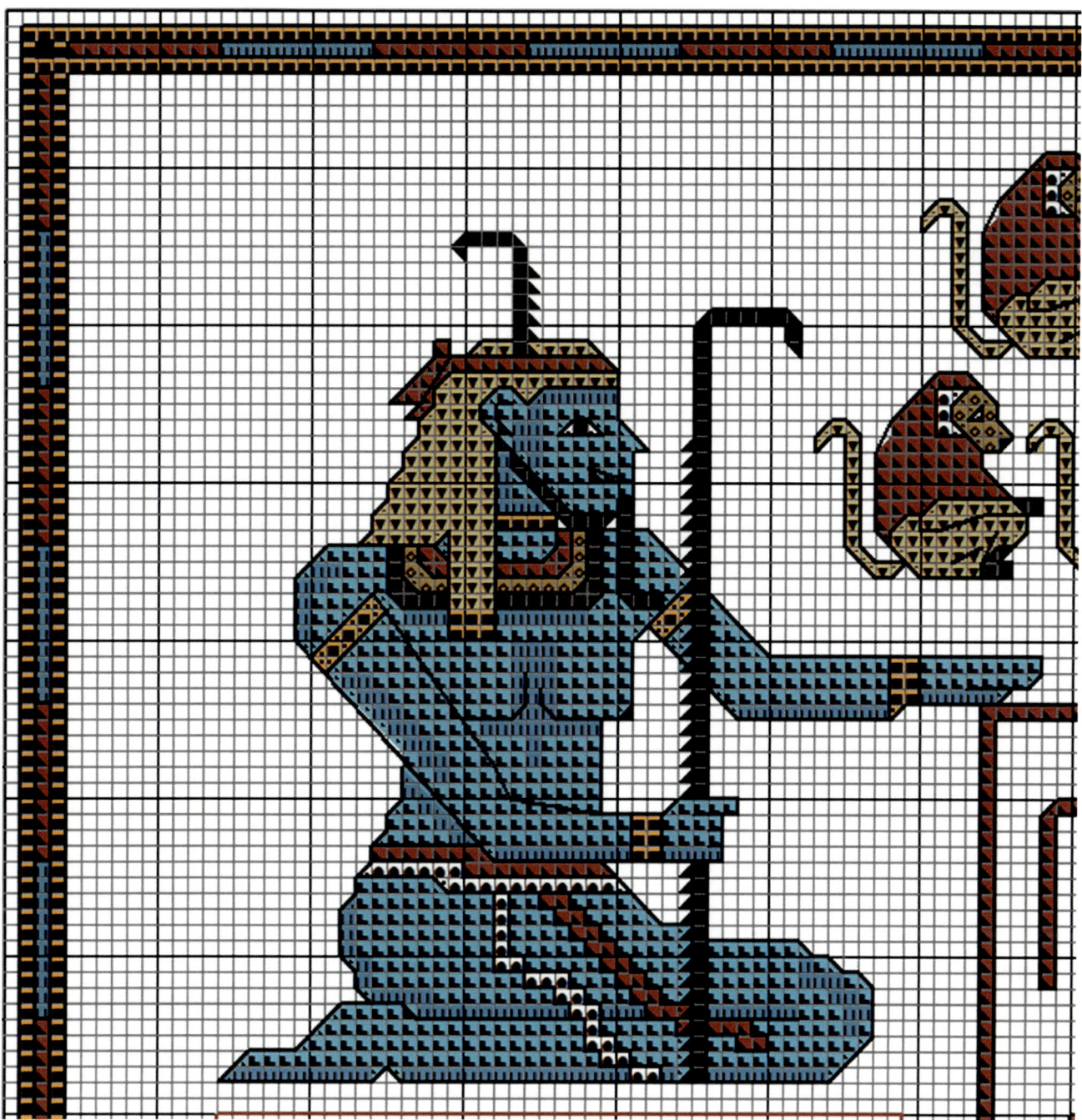

Egyptian Sampler Section 1

Juliet Foster

Egyptian Sampler Section 2

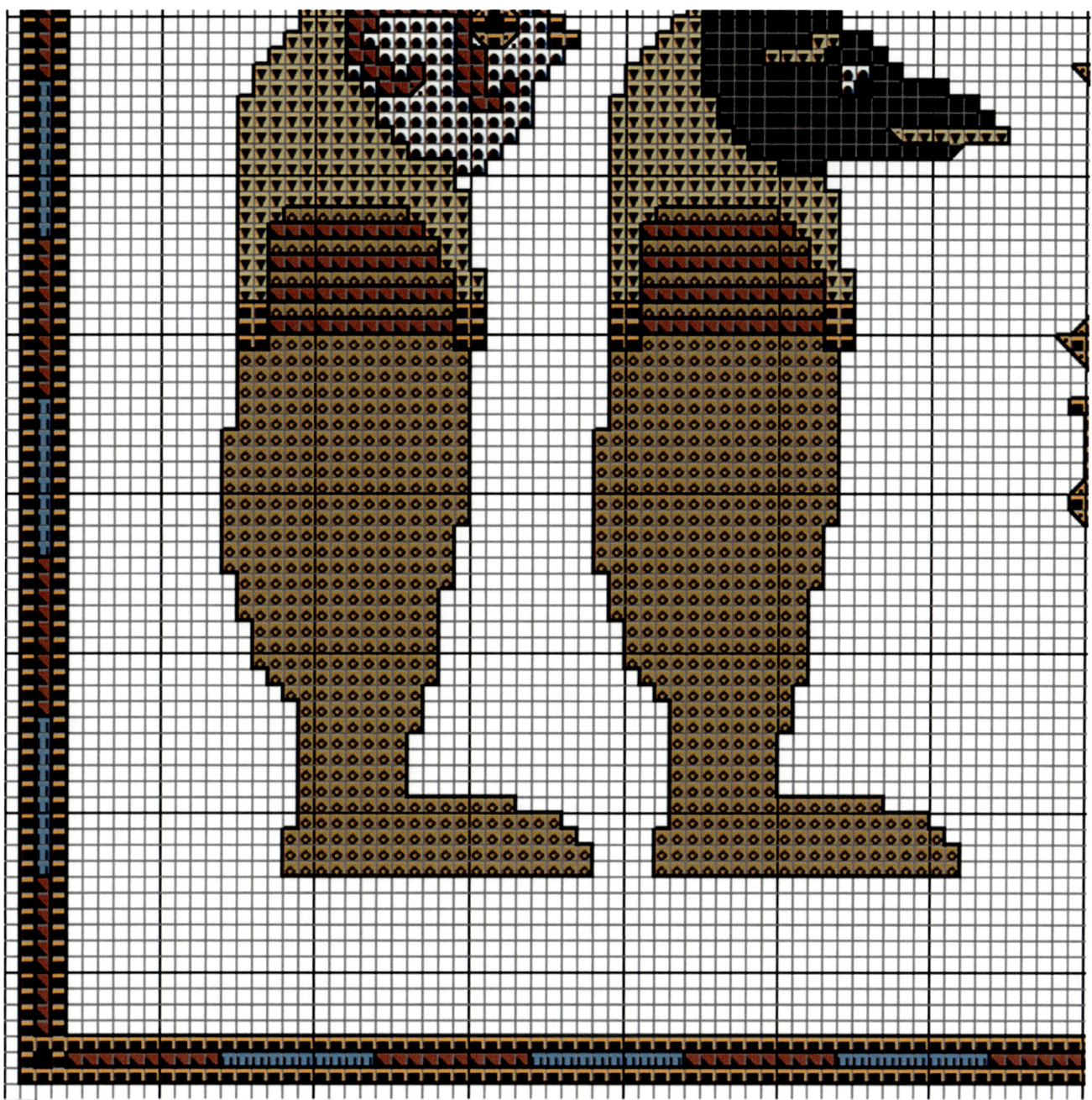

Egyptian Sampler Section 3

Juliet Foster

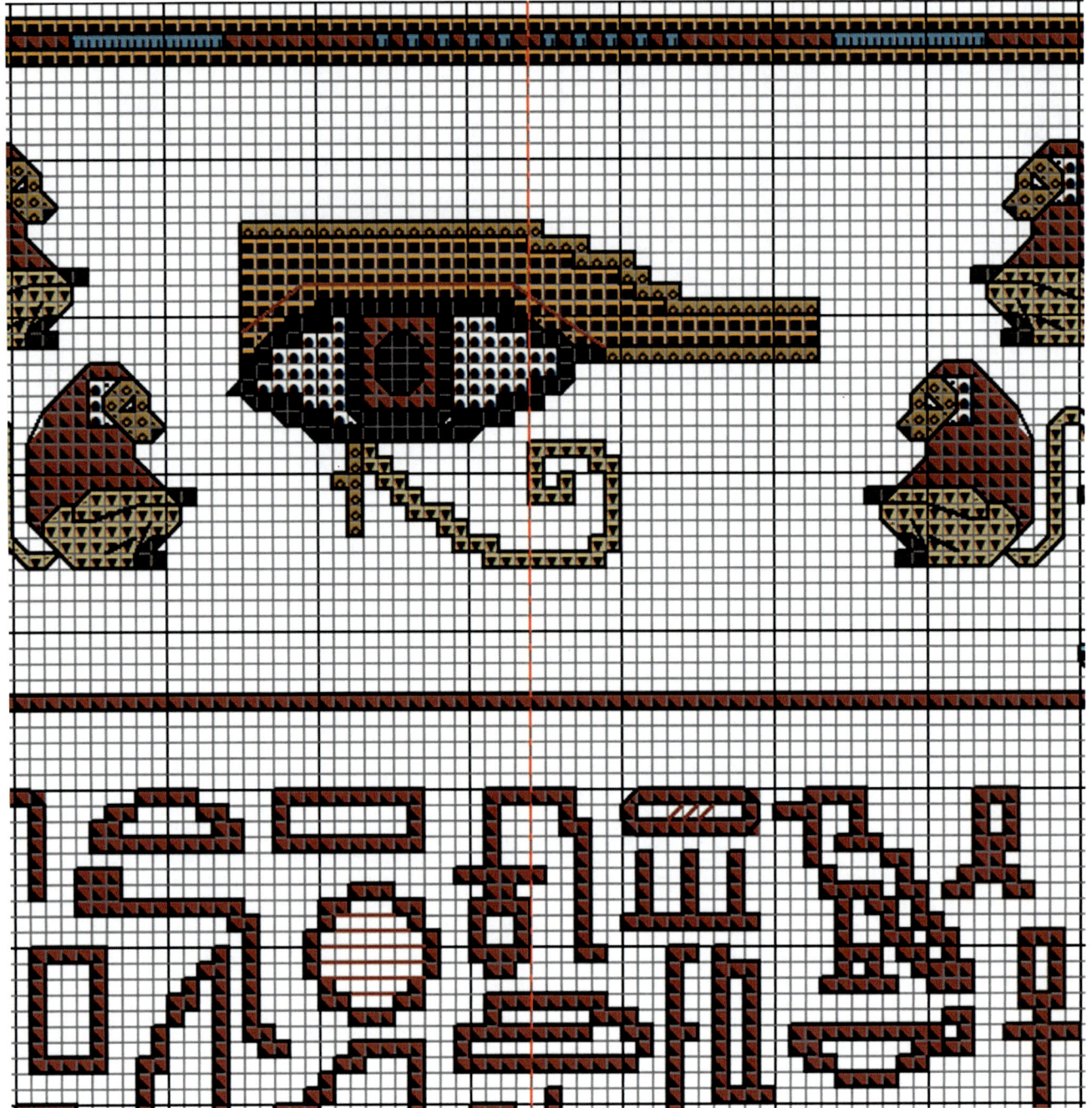

Egyptian Sampler Section 4

Egyptian Sampler Section 5

Juliet Foster

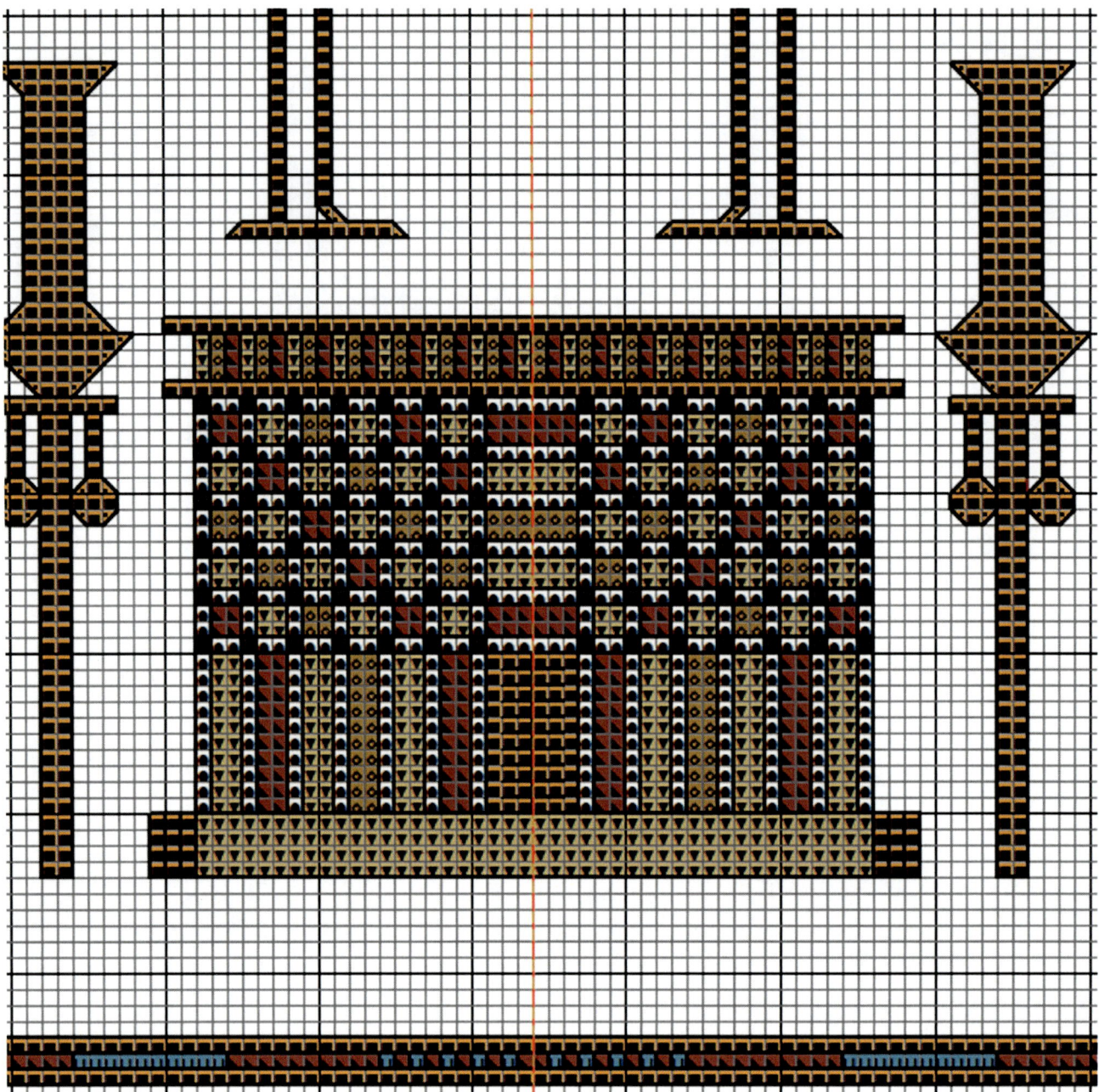

Egyptian Sampler Section 6

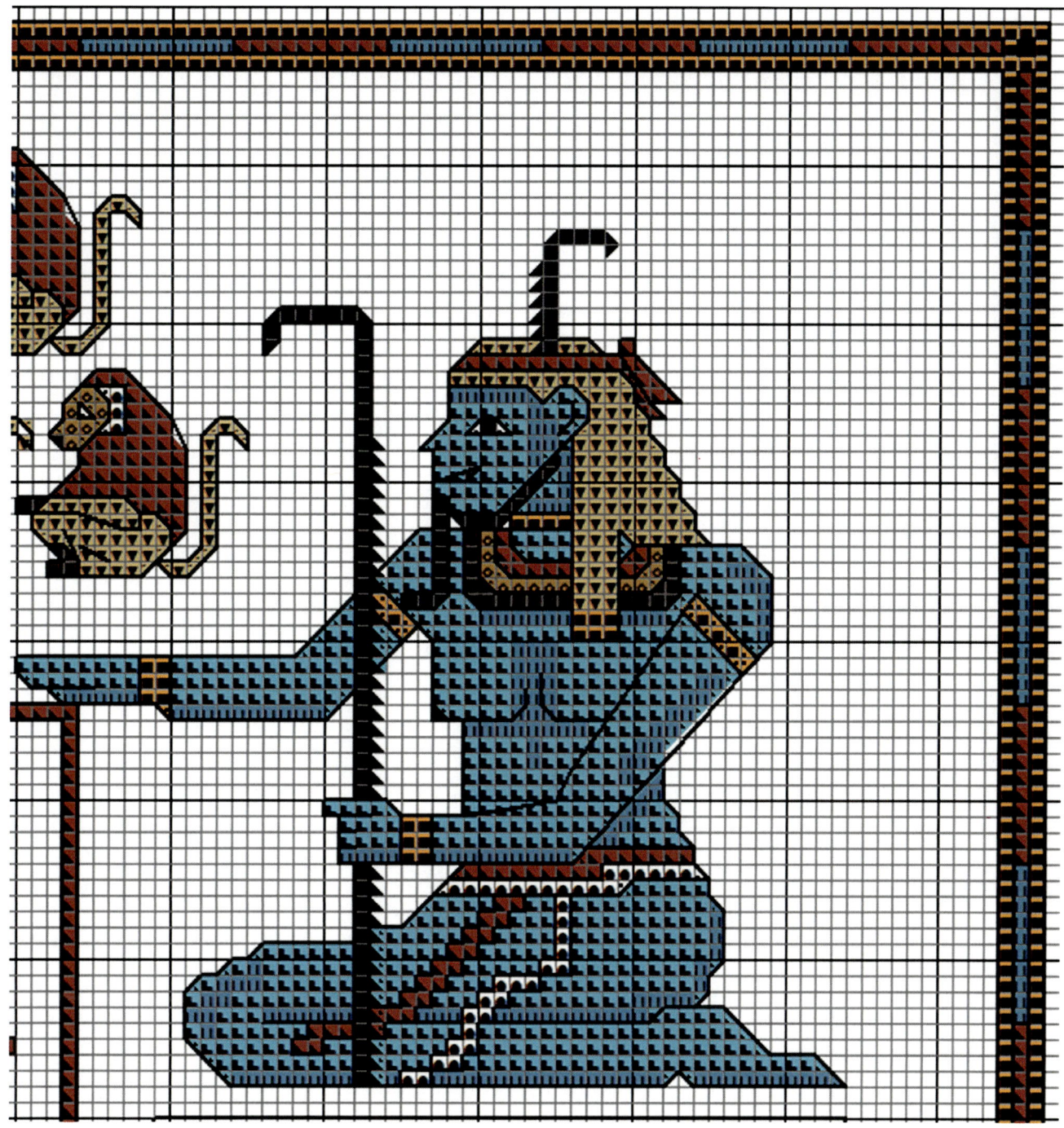

Egyptian Sampler Section 7

Juliet Foster

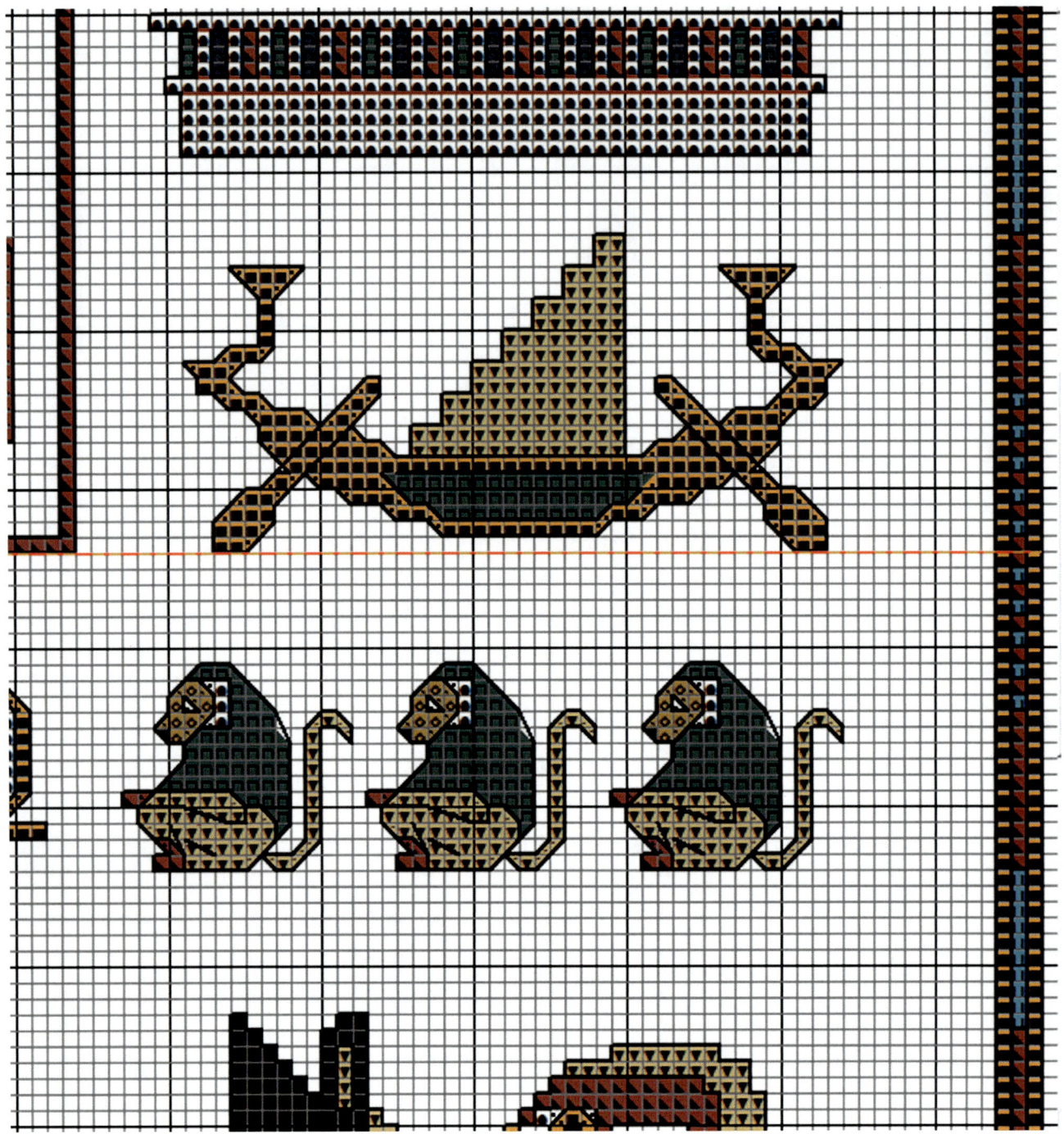

Egyptian Sampler Section 8

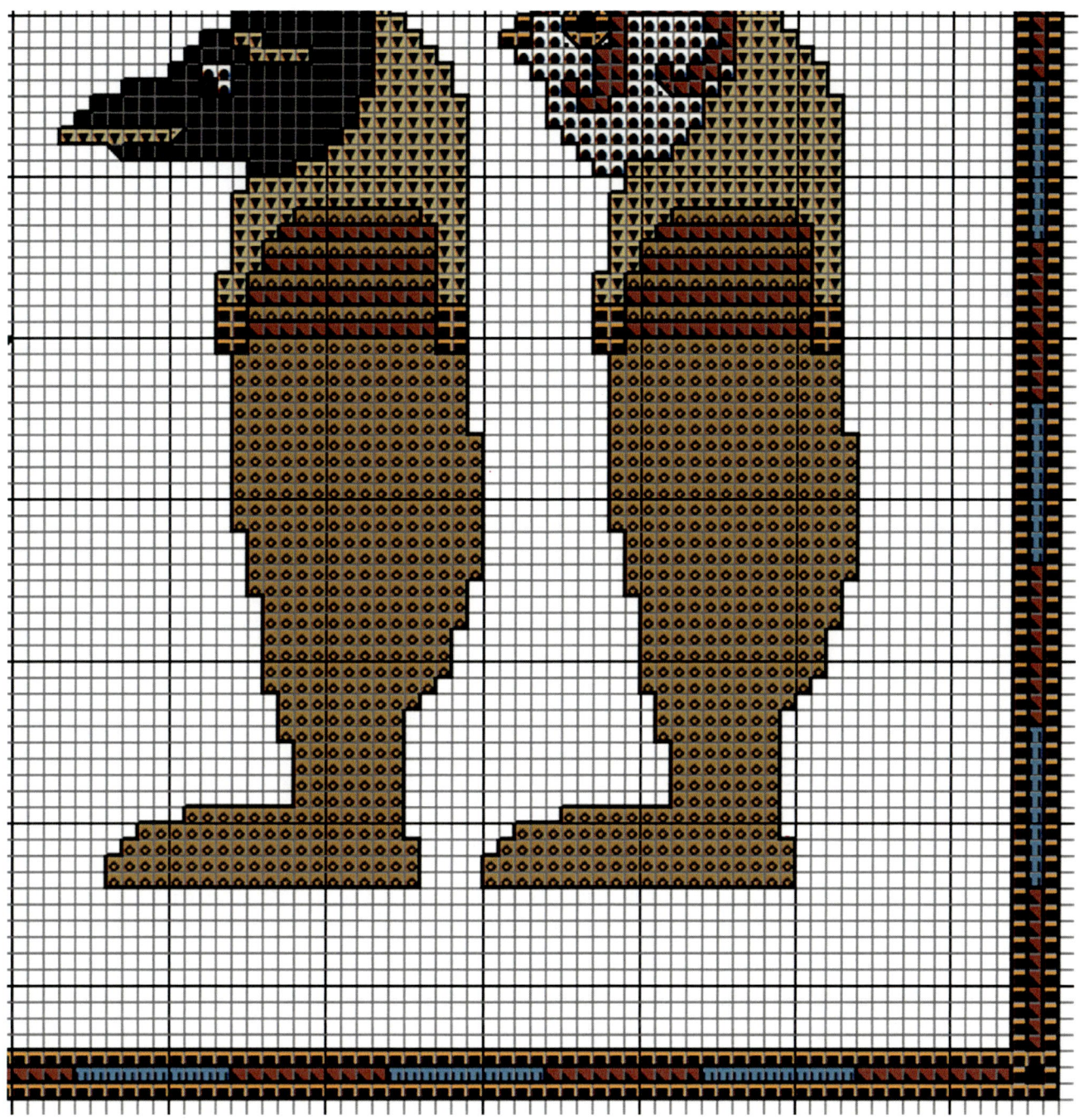

Egyptian Sampler Section 9

Juliet Foster

What is MS?

MS or multiple sclerosis is a neurological condition affecting around 100,000 people in the UK alone. That's enough to fill Wembley Stadium to capacity and still have ten thousand people left outside. Most people are diagnosed between the ages of 20-40, but it can affect younger and older people too. Almost twice as many women have MS than men.

No-one knows for sure what causes MS, but it's likely that a combination of genetic and environmental factors play a role.

When someone develops MS, it stays with them for life. Treatments and specialists can help to manage the symptoms, but as yet they can't be stopped. MS works against the central nervous system – the brain, spinal column and optic nerve – causing a range of symptoms. Everyone with MS is different.
It works by triggering the body's own immune system to attack the protective coating around the nerves, called myelin. Nerves are a bit like the wiring of your house – electrical cable surrounded by a protective covering. If you imagine something chips away at the coating exposing the wires and affecting the electrical signals, you have a pretty good idea of what MS does to the body.

Depending on which part of the central nervous system the MS attacks, different symptoms can occur. One time it might be blindness, another time it might be vertigo. Symptoms can last for days, weeks, months, sometimes longer. Having one symptom does not rule out having others at the same time.
There is no way to predict what will happen next – patients just have to wait and see.

Over time the condition is debilitating because damage to the central nervous system builds up. In some people this is quite mild. In others it's devastating. New treatments are always under development that can slow down the progression of the condition, but as yet there is no cure.

Thank you for buying this book. Every penny donated to MS research and support is well spent. The proceeds from this chart, once they reach a level where royalties are paid, are given to the MS Society who channel funds into all of the aspects of MS, from advising patients to funding specialist nurses to vital research.

Other publications in this range

Eye of Horus – Egyptian Collection Counted Cross Stitch (Kindle edition)
Heh, god of Mischief – Egyptian Collection Counted Cross Stitch (Kindle edition)
Ibis and Baboon – Egyptian Collection Counted Cross Stitch (Kindle edition)

Made in United States
Orlando, FL
16 May 2024